The **Joy** *of* **You**

The Joy of You

Your Life After Divorce

William E. Rabior, ACSW

Liguori
ONE LIGUORI DRIVE
LIGUORI MO 63057-9999

Imprimi Potest:
Thomas D. Picton, C.Ss.R.
Provincial, Denver Province
The Redemptorists

Published by Liguori Publications
Liguori, Missouri
To order, call 800-325-9521
www.liguori.org

Library of Congress Cataloging-in-Publication Data

Rabior, William E.
  The joy of you : your life after divorce / William E. Rabior.—1st ed.
     p. cm.
  ISBN 978-0-7648-1853-0
  1. Divorced people—Religious life. 2. Divorce—Religious aspects—Catholic Church. I. Title.
  BV4596.D58R33 2010
  248.8'46—dc22

                                                                        2009037383

Liguori Publications, a nonprofit corporation, is an apostolate of the Redemptorists. To learn more about the Redemptorists, visit Redemptorists.com.

Printed in the United States of America
14 13 12 11 10   5 4 3 2 1
First edition

*I dedicate this book
to my wife, Susan, and my daughter, Gabrielle.
You are the sunshine of my life.*

Table of Contents

―――――

Introduction

———

It was my friend, Jim, who a few years ago gave me the idea for this book. Jim is a relationship counselor who has been in the field a long time. He has walked with numerous couples through the sweetness and the sorrow, the good times and the bad, through new beginnings and final endings. One day over coffee, he made an observation which stuck in my mind. It went like this:

"At the risk of oversimplifying, it seems to me that once a marriage ends in a divorce, two groups of people emerge. There are those who survive the divorce but never fully heal afterwards. They tend to be the walking wounded who just can't seem to recover or move on with their lives. The second group is made up of those who not only survive, but after a while start to thrive. Their life 'AD' (After Divorce) is often actually better than 'BC' (Before Collapse). It may not be right away, and it goes beyond remarriage. They find a renewed sense of spiritual and emotional equilibrium. They redefine themselves if necessary and manage to successfully rebuild themselves and their lives. They turn their divorce experience into what I call 'positive failure.' They learn from it and keep right on growing. It's a nice thing to see." He added, "Whenever I meet someone like that, I always am curious about how they did it, and generally I ask them what helped the most. I'll bet you do, too."

I nodded in agreement. Having done a considerable amount of relationship counseling myself, I knew what he meant. But with that conversation, Jim got me thinking. What are the factors that help bring about successful healing following a divorce? Are there certain paths that lead to new wholeness and others that torpedo the process? What works and what doesn't?

And so I began a process of reflection and analysis based on numerous conversations I had with persons who found healing after the trauma of divorce, and over time, this book took shape.

I was able to distill eight factors (I call them "paths") which are instrumental in the healing process. There are very likely others, but these tended to be most prominent in the interviews I conducted.

Respecting the privacy and confidentiality of those interviewed was of paramount concern to me. I have been careful to protect the identity of everyone I spoke to, so actual names are never used unless the persons gave me permission to use their real names in describing their experiences.

This intentionally is not a long book. It is written for busy persons who may not have a lot of time for reading but who are nonetheless interested in exploring dynamics that have proven helpful to others and that may provide healing insights to the reader. Acquiring these insights may lead you to pursue them in a more in-depth fashion, for example, through therapy or counseling.

Some brief advice: Allow yourself to be open to new kinds of healing modalities. If necessary, give yourself permission to jettison old ways of thinking and acting which no longer work. Give yourself permission to change and grow. Above all, give yourself permission to heal. Unless you do, it will not happen.

If this book helps move you closer to your own healing, even in some small way, then it is worth all the time and effort I put into it. As you read, pray for guidance and direction, then listen to your inner voices speaking to you about your experiences with divorce.

Above all, strive to hear the voice of God. God talks to us more often than we realize, and coming to new wholeness is dependent upon listening to what God tells us and choosing the paths he directs us to walk.

We cannot walk every path, and some are more important than others when it comes to our healing. Only God can show us which ways to go—which paths are best for us.

On your journey, may your trials turn into triumphs, and may you move steadily from pain to peace. May your struggles become stepping stones to a future full of hope, and may your burdens be transformed into bridges to new possibilities that are rich with promise. May you come to know the joy of being you. Be patient with yourself and expect the best. I believe you will get it.

What Does It Mean
to Heal After a Divorce?

––––––

Most persons who divorce will be in need of some kind of healing—emotional, psychological, spiritual, or more likely, all three. Of course, people experience divorce in different ways, tailored to their own personality, their life situation, and other circumstances. The level of hurt or woundedness and the corresponding need for healing differ with each person. For some, the need is great. For others, it may be less so.

There is no such thing as a cookie-cutter or one-size-fits-all experience of either divorce or healing, because everyone is unique. Nor does healing involve some kind of journey toward perfection or a trouble-free life. The goal of healing is not to become perfect, but to become more whole, more together, happier, and more peace-filled.

How do you heal, then, following a divorce? In my conversations with those who have divorced, I invariably asked that question and received a wide variety of responses. Each response reflected the person's unique experiences with divorce and how those experiences impacted his or her life's journey. Gena, Lynne, and Larry shared with me their insights into healing and how that process unfolded in their lives.

"I was married twenty years," Gena said. "On our twentieth anniversary, my husband told me he no longer loved me and wanted a divorce. He later remarried a woman who was half his age."

What happened next? "I disintegrated. I fell apart completely," Gena told me. She described the experience as the "proverbial nervous breakdown," during which she could barely function. The breakdown lasted several months and was severe enough that she was hospitalized. Yet during our conversation, Gena looked self-possessed and very much at peace with herself and her life. She had obviously moved past the trauma of the divorce to a calm place. I asked her about healing.

"The first thing I need to say about healing is that for me it has been a process, not an event. I prayed very hard to God to take away my pain, but that didn't happen instantaneously, like I wanted it to. It happened gradually, over time. Healing requires time. The greater your sense of loss, the more time is needed. The second thing about healing is that it is hard to do all by yourself. I tried, but early on, I realized I needed help."

Where did she find help? Gina credited a year of counseling and the support group sponsored by her parish. "I needed someone to listen to me as I vented my rage and feelings of betrayal. I found good listeners in both my counselor and the group. They listened without judging me," she explained.

Gina's healing came about when she realized her marriage was over, but her life was not. Knowing that she still had much to do and much to give, Gena came to another important realization: "I began to see, above all, that my failed marriage did not make me a failure." The final phase of healing came when she was actually able to forgive her ex-husband for what happened.

"Without a doubt," Gena told me, "I forgave him and I meant it. More than anything else, that is what set me free."

Lynne's divorce experience came at a pretty bad time in her life. Yet today, even at the supermarket, Lynne possesses such an aura of serenity that other shoppers often pause and look at her face. I knew, however, that she hadn't always been that way.

"I was married ten years to an alcoholic who was also abusive—verbally and physically," she said. "There were days in the summertime when I went to work wearing a long-sleeve shirt to cover the bruises on my arms. We had two children together, and I could see that they, too, were getting hurt by what was happening in my marriage. But I didn't know what to do. Only prayer helped me make it through the day."

What changed things? Lynne believes that God heard her prayers and sent an angel. "She didn't have wings, but she had a compassionate heart and a keen sense of observation. I'm talking about my boss at work." Sensing something was wrong, Lynne's boss gently coaxed the truth out of her. "I told her everything," Lynne happily admits. That night Lynne and her children were able, with her boss's help, to stay in a shelter for abused women. Eventually, those at the shelter helped her file for a divorce, but more importantly, Lynne said, "They steered me toward a new life."

What helped her heal? Lynne was able to move to a new city and start over. In hindsight, she understands that her self-confidence was low because of all the abuse. Her reliance on God made a difference. "I asked God for help, and he provided it once again. I joined a wonderful parish and began to go to Mass every day. I came to view the Eucharist as the great sacrament of healing. Through it, Christ touched my mind and heart. More than anything else, his love healed me, so I was able to become strong in the broken places. If you see something in my face, it is his peace, and I thank him for it every day."

Larry also told me his story. At eighteen, he had married the young woman carrying his child. "Our families put a lot of pressure on the two of us to get married. It seemed like a good solution for the problems created by the pregnancy. We didn't love each other, but we liked each other, and we thought that would be enough." He shook his head. "It wasn't."

From the beginning of the marriage, Larry said, they began to drift apart. They lived separate lives, with separate friends and separate activities. Looking back, he described the situation as "two lives that never seemed to intersect or become one." When she filed for divorce after five years of marriage, they were nearly strangers to one another; yet they still "liked" each other.

What were the healing issues? "Feeling guilty about many things, including the pregnancy and my inability to make the marriage work," said Larry. He tried to invest more of himself in the relationship, believing that it would make things different. He met with his pastor, "a wonderful priest with a counseling background." Through these meetings, Larry was able to work through the guilt issues. His pastor recommended that Larry begin the process toward a Church annulment. Larry thought this was a good idea, because he still hoped to meet the "right" person and marry again.

Larry beamed and showed me his wedding ring. "We've been married nearly seven years now, and our marriage gets better every day. I guess you could say I'm living proof that there is life after divorce."

A constellation of signs that healing is taking place have evolved from my many conversations with persons who have experienced divorce and have made great progress toward healing:

- You begin to have more good days than bad days.
- You can actually talk about your former spouse and the marriage without breaking down and crying.
- You may still love or like your former spouse, but you no longer feel emotionally tied to her or him. This is sometimes referred to as completing the "emotional divorce."
- You no longer panic about being alone.
- Remarriage may be an option, but so is remaining single.
- You stop dreading the holidays or special days like your anniversary.
- You begin to successfully manage your emotions, particularly anger, instead of your emotions managing you.
- You pray for your former spouse.
- You no longer act depressed.
- You begin to enjoy the present and start planning for your future.
- You laugh more frequently.
- You listen with compassion and understanding to others who have divorced. You help as best you can.
- You no longer have revenge-filled thoughts about your former spouse or look for ways to get even.
- You start to feel self-confident.
- You feel thankful.
- You begin to ask yourself what you can learn from your experience of divorce, and you even see some good things coming from it that may not have been evident before.

- You have peace in your heart, and it radiates into every aspect of your life, including your relationship with your former spouse.
- You feel healed inside.

Our need for healing is ongoing and can manifest itself differently over time. Since we live in an imperfect world, our healing, too, might not be perfect. There very likely will be times when you may slip back into old ways of thinking and acting. At such times, ask God for help and guidance, reaffirm what you have already achieved, and work on regaining your balance.

You know full well that the paths of negativity you once walked need to be left behind. They offer nothing to you anymore, and walking them again may only cause you to lose your way.

Right now, nothing is more important than your healing and whatever aspects of it you achieve. Claim them as your own, hold fast to them, and let them gift you in all the ways they can. Healing is something you deserve, so do whatever you need to achieve it. It can happen. Make it happen. Make it part of the joy of being you.

Things to Think About

1. Have you given yourself permission to heal from your divorce? If not, why not?
2. In what area of your life do you most need healing right now?
3. What are you going to do about it?

The
Eight Paths

Doing Your Grief Work:
A Path to Healing

———

Generally speaking, with a divorce comes grieving, sometimes the deepest grieving a person has ever experienced. There are many different kinds of death, and the death of a marriage can feel as devastating as the death of a loved one—sometimes even more so. Whenever we lose something or someone very important to us, we are likely to grieve.

When this happens, we will grieve in our own way, at our own speed, influenced by our unique personality and our past life experiences of loss. Although people share common grief-associated denominators, no one grieves in exactly the same way as another person.

"The day I was served my divorce papers," said Rick, "my mother died totally unexpectedly. So it was a double blow that left me reeling. To say I was a mess is the understatement of the century. For a time, I simply couldn't function. I just wanted to crawl in bed, pull the covers over my head, and sleep, and for awhile, that is exactly what I did. I knew that I was grieving for both my marriage and my mom, but everything converged, and after awhile I couldn't separate the grief for one from the other. I felt so overwhelmed that I knew I needed help. The company I work for has an employee assistance program, and they allowed me to see a counselor for a few sessions. When those ran out, I paid for additional counseling out of my own pocket. It was worth every penny. After awhile, I started to get a handle on my grieving and move toward grief recovery."

Allen said: "Even though I knew my marriage was over, and nothing more could be done to save it, and even though I'm the one who filed for divorce, my grief was still so strong it surprised me. I started to experience intense mood swings that I had never had before. For example, I would go from sad to mad to glad in about five minutes, then start all over again. To make matters worse, I began to drink more, which made the sadness and feelings of depression even worse. I was really hurting. Then I read a book on grief that said you can't heal what you don't feel. That day I made a decision to stop anesthetizing myself with alcohol and start allowing myself to feel my grief no matter how bad it got. And, believe me, it did get bad. For awhile I thought I couldn't do it, but then I noticed the inner pain becoming less. I began to feel better and actually started having a few good days again. I knew I had made it through the emotional tornado and that I would be OK." Allen smiled. "And I am."

Grieving is not an event; it is a process that can affect us physically, emotionally, and even spiritually. Physically, for example, a grieving person may experience a variety of somatic complaints such as headaches, weight loss, insomnia, and even body pain.

Emotionally, grief can give rise to anxiety, depression, and guilt. Grieving associated with divorce can also impact a person's spiritual life, as Charlene's story illustrates:

"My divorce triggered a spiritual reaction that I never saw coming, but I guess I should have," she said. "I have always suffered from low self-esteem and would often beat myself up for what I saw as failures and inadequacies on my part. Once I got divorced, I started believing that God himself was going to beat me up—that he would punish me for ending my marriage because he was so angry at me. It got so bad and so irrational that I stopped going to church, because I viewed myself as a terrible, horrible person. I just knew that God didn't want me in his house.

"Fortunately for me, I have a truly wonderful pastor. He stopped in to see me one day, because he noticed my absence at Mass and wondered if something was wrong. He was literally a godsend. By that I mean God sent him to me. I poured out my heart to him, and he just listened. Then he showed me how my grieving had become impaired and was damaging me. We celebrated the sacrament of reconciliation together, and he gave me absolution. That was the turning point and the beginning of my healing.

"When I was alienated from God, the spiritual pain and loneliness were unbearable. For me, Grief Land is a dark and horrible place I never ever want to return to."

Grief can be extraordinarily painful, yet it is not our enemy. It is, in fact, our ally that enables us to heal following a great personal loss such as the end of a marriage.

Denial, anger, bargaining, depression, and acceptance are usually cited as the five stages of grieving. However, experts are increasingly in agreement that there are actually no stages at all. Instead, there are five phases or responses that grieving individuals revisit over and over again, often for a very long time.

Other experts describe the grief process as having three components. The first is shock—the feeling that this (divorce) cannot be happening to me. The second is a feeling of disintegration—the world I have known is now falling apart. The third is reintegration—coming back together and finding the strength to live with the loss.

However it is described, grieving is hard work. It is an arduous process that forms and transforms us forever. It can make us better or bitter. The choice is up to us.

Grief studies suggest that women and men tend to handle loss differently. Women, for example, often have better social-support systems, especially through close friends. Usually, they turn to them when they are grieving in an effort to regain their emotional balance.

Men, on the other hand, often tend to keep their grief to themselves—bottling it up, suppressing, or denying it. It is not uncommon for a grieving man to turn to alcohol to ease his emotional pain. Or he may lose himself in a flurry of activity, for example, escaping into his work to avoid having to face his grief. Avoiding or putting off grieving usually means having to face it later on in life.

Resolving our grieving issues or recovering from our grief is done by doing the necessary grief work. We heal from grief by grieving. The aim of grief work is not to erase the memories of what we have experienced so that we become amnesiacs who can no longer recall an important part of our personal history. Rather, it is to make those memories less painfully controlling and disturbing. It is how we finally achieve some level of peace after the emotional and spiritual storms that often accompany an event like divorce.

Grief work is seldom a once-and-for-all event. It tends to be repetitive. Usually, we need to face our grief and express our feelings related to it over and over, until the inner turmoil starts to dissipate and we come to a place of acceptance. Acceptance does not mean we necessarily approve of what has happened, but we know now that the marriage is truly over, and there is nothing more we can do about it.

It is now time to begin moving forward and living our life without our former spouse. It is time for what is sometimes referred to as creating a "new normal"—a new and different way of being in this world that we gradually grow to accept and adapt to.

Grief work for many divorced persons is one of the hardest things they have ever had to face. It is so difficult and demanding that the temptation is to ignore it, hoping the grief will go away. It may or may not.

The fact is that ignoring our grief may prove to be damaging to our well-being. Unresolved grief can destabilize our life and take a toll on our peace of mind. It can affect us in ways we may not even recognize. That is what happened to Leo.

"After twenty-eight years of marriage, my wife filed for divorce. I went into shock, and that was replaced very quickly by anger. Actually, anger is not a strong enough word. It was more like fury. I am not a violent person, but there were times when I became so furious, I wished her dead. I was so angry at her that I wouldn't talk to her for two years. All communication was through either my attorney or through our three kids.

He continued. "Those three kids eventually saved my sanity and maybe my soul. They did a kind of intervention with me. They sat me down and told me all the things they had observed in me—how my anger was poisoning every aspect of my life and spilling over beyond me to them. They said that unless and until I dealt with it, the entire family would continue to suffer.

"At first I resisted, but they had planted seeds in my head. I asked my doctor for help soon after that, and she directed me to an anger management group. I stayed with that group for over a year, and it helped change my attitudes about the divorce. I can't say I am anger-free, but my outbursts are fewer and fewer, and I actually have begun talking to my former wife and even praying for her." Leo chuckled. "For me that really is progress."

When it comes to grief work, probably the single best way to process our grief is to talk it out with someone we trust. We have to be able to feel comfortable enough and safe enough with her or him to be able to share our deepest feelings and most private thoughts. This individual may be a close friend, a clergy person, or a professional counselor. Later in this book, we will discuss the benefits of professional therapy.

Many churches and communities also have support groups for those trying to cope with a divorce. These are different from bereavement support groups made up of those grieving the actual death of a loved one. Support groups can provide valuable assistance free-of-charge. You not only get to vent your own feelings, but in addition, you can see how others are coping and what has proven helpful in their quest for healing.

Try putting your true feelings down on paper. Start journaling or writing letters to your former spouse (don't mail them), to God, to yourself, to your children, to anyone at all. You can share your regrets, how you really feel, and things you wish you had said. Writing has helped many grieving persons find solace and can also provide you with valuable insights that may prove helpful to your healing process.

The idea behind doing grief work is to keep the healing process moving until a more whole and calmer state is reached. Sometimes, however, the process stops altogether, or persons become frozen in their grief and disabled by it, usually because of such factors as debilitating mental illness like depression and anxiety or alcohol and drug abuse.

At such times, professional help is recommended. Asking for help is never a sign of weakness. It is in fact a sign that the grieving person wants to move beyond crippling personal pain to a better, happier, and more fulfilling way of life—something God desires for each of us.

In conclusion, grief recovery after a divorce takes place when we know it is time to move on with our lives. We deliberately choose to become survivors and not victims. No one can tell us how long to grieve or when to stop. Generally, we will know when it is time. Grief carried on too long can become unhealthy to us. It can sap our energy and drain away the strength we need to function well and live a decent life.

When you realize that you are growing into a healthier, freer, more independent, and more joyous you, take these as signs of grief recovery. You are healing, and it is truly something to celebrate.

Things to Think About

1. Are you still grieving for your marriage? If so, where do you think you are in the grieving process?
2. If you are frozen in your grief, do you need help? If you do, will you seek it soon?
3. Is there more grief work to be done? If so, what remains?

Befriending Your Anger

Ron was a talented story teller. At the divorce support group called New Beginnings, whenever he illustrated a point about divorce with a story, the group listened with rapt attention.

"Tonight, I'd like to tell you a brief story about anger," he told the group one winter's evening. "I wish I could take credit for it, but it was originally told by the Native Americans. It seems that a wise old grandfather was trying to instruct his grandson about human nature. 'In the deepest part of every human person,' the old man began, 'there live two animals. The first is gentle and kind. It has a good heart and always strives to be peaceful and compassionate. The second has an evil heart and is warlike and cruel. It enjoys sowing the seeds of dissension and likes to see suffering and misery.'

" 'Well, then,' asked the boy, 'which animal is more powerful?' The grandfather looked into his eyes and replied, 'The one that you feed, my child, the one that you feed.' "

Ron paused for a moment to let the point sink home. Then he continued. "I think it is crucial to stop feeding the anger coming from our divorce, and instead, befriend it so that it works for us and not against us." Then, he sat down. That meeting was held over fifteen years ago, and I still remember both the story and the point that he made so well.

Anger is probably the most misunderstood and under-appreciated of all the emotions. Enough things have been written about anger to fill dozens of libraries. Much is very likely true, but much is not, because the emotion itself tends to be looked at and interpreted negatively when in fact it has positive attributes.

First of all, anger is a normal, healthy emotion. God in his wisdom has made it a part of our emotional makeup. He has given the potential for anger to every human being, and so it is a gift. Like any of his gifts, he invites us to use it wisely and well, and that is precisely the challenge for all of us.

The fact is that for many of us, anger is a difficult emotion to manage or control. It has a way of turning the tables on us so that after awhile, it becomes our master and begins managing and controlling us. For this reason, then, a little bit of anger goes a very long way in a marriage. The same could be said about divorce.

Anger provides a signal that something is wrong—perhaps seriously wrong—and needs attention. The challenge for us is to accurately decipher the message without destroying the messenger or ourselves.

If we lose the ability to control our anger, then we may very well become just another casualty of its ability to wreak havoc in our lives or in the lives of others. On the other hand, if we choose to befriend it, we can actually harness its power to work in our favor.

Here is some of Diane's story: "I never wanted a divorce, but I got one anyway. We were married seven years. I knew we had drifted apart somewhat, but I didn't think it was all that serious. Then one day I came home from work, and he had moved out. He left me a note saying that our differences were irreconcilable and that he intended to file for divorce immediately.

"I begged him to give our marriage one more chance. I pointed out to him that we hadn't even attempted counseling, but he insisted that there was nothing more that could be to done to save it, and so file he did.

"It's been said that hurting people hurt people, and that describes my reaction to the divorce. I was so hurt and furious that all I wanted to do was hurt him in any way I could. I spent the next three years doing just that, especially by using our two small children as pawns in a game I played with him. He got hurt, but he also retaliated, and I got hurt. It was a lose-lose situation.

"Then one day I bumped into an old college friend I hadn't seen in years. We went to lunch, and I told her what had happened to my marriage and to me. She shared the story of her divorce, which took place about the same time mine did. The thing is, she looked pretty peaceful, and I didn't detect any anger at all.

"My friend laughed. 'Oh, I had plenty of rage, and I did my best to make his life miserable. Then one day it's as though a light went on in my soul. I knew that I had had enough of living that way. So I got angry at my anger! *You don't get to push me around anymore,* I informed it. That day I channeled my anger-energy into a vigorous run. The next day I did the same thing but ran a little farther. Soon, I was running five miles a day, then seven, then ten. I ran in the sun, the rain, even the snow. I ran to reclaim my life,' she told me."

Diane smiled. "Long story short is that I did the same thing. I channeled my anger into something I had always wanted to do. I painted my house from top to bottom. It looked so good, and I received so many compliments, that I had an 'aha' moment of inspiration and decided to start my own business painting houses. I now employ five painters, and four of them are divorced women who are learning to use their anger in a useful way like I learned to do."

The fact is that anger can fuel action. If we befriend it, it can actually energize us and propel us to work toward achieving important goals. The choice is always ours to make.

I asked the divorced women and men whom I interviewed to share their experience with anger surrounding their divorce and to tell me if their anger in any way became their friend or ally in the healing process.

It was interesting to me to discover that almost all the persons who described themselves as having achieved considerable healing in their lives following divorce had also learned to use their anger positively—in other words, to befriend it. For most of them, though, it was not an easy process. Eddy, Dennis, and Nadine described their experiences this way.

"After my divorce," said Eddy, "I honestly felt for a time that I had a demon living inside of me—that's how powerful the anger had become. Every time I got angry at my ex-wife, it seemed to grow even stronger. How do you get rid of a demon? You need God's help, so I sought out a priest and asked him to pray over me and order that dark force to leave me. He did, and it did. The priest suggested that I clean house while I was at it and get rid of more negative debris. He taught me how to meditate by focusing on my breathing. Now, when I start to feel angry, I just breathe out the anger and breathe in God's peace. It's a simple technique that really works well for me. In the process of getting rid of my anger, I actually have ended up growing closer to God. It shows how God can bring goodness even out of evil."

Dennis explained: "I felt that much of the anger I experienced from my divorce was justified. In other words, I had a right to be angry, but I knew I didn't have a right to be cruel, and that's what I saw happening to me. I would use every chance I had to stick it to my former wife and even to my kids, who chose to live with her. My righteous anger was becoming toxic to me, and I came to the conclusion that I had to do something about it. For one thing, I had too much time on my hands, and I used it to rehash the divorce over and over. So what did I do to change things? I joined the local chapter of Habitat for Humanity. Now, instead of getting a pounding headache from my anger, I pound nails and help people. It works for me."

"To me," said Nadine, "the notion of befriending your anger after your divorce seems strange, because for a long time—at least four years—my anger was my enemy. My whole life was steeped in anger. I knew it, but I didn't know what to do about it. After my husband left me, anger was a whole-body event. My insides felt like they were tied up in knots, I had headaches almost daily, and my blood pressure was dangerously high. Most of the time I just felt sick, and I knew it was from the anger. It was killing me."

How did things change for her? "I was healed by love. My children were grown, and I lived alone, so my sister suggested I become a foster mother. I had some fears and doubts at first, but when I saw the little disabled child who was going to be placed with me, my heart melted, and I fell in love again. That was ten years ago, and I'm proud to say that during that time, sixteen children have been placed with me. I gave each one all the love I could give, and the more I loved them, the better I felt. After awhile, I realized I wasn't angry at my former husband anymore. The Bible says that love drives out fear. In my case, it also drove out my anger, or maybe it's more accurate to say that my anger was transformed into love. At the time of my divorce, I never thought I would ever be happy again, but God is full of surprises. Thanks to all the beautiful children whom I have been privileged to care for, I've been surprised by joy."

In the normal circumstances of daily living, anger can be difficult to control and manage. Add to the ordinary stresses of life the super stress which comes from a divorce, and your coping skills may be tested to the limit.

You probably have been hurt by your divorce (some more than others). You may be fully justified in feeling angry. Just remember that even justifiable anger takes a toll on a person's mind, body, and spirit.

The fact is that our body does not know the difference between good anger and bad anger. All it knows is that we are angry, and it responds accordingly with physiological stress responses that over time create wear and tear on our whole person.

The Bible says not to let the sun go down on your anger, and that is good advice, because when the sun does go down on unresolved anger, it will be there in the morning ready to make your life miserable with another day of hurt and pain.

Befriending your anger calls for an honest assessment of what you are really feeling, as well as a creative look at your needs and resources. It has been said that anger is the beginning of courage. Allowing your anger to become your friend may mean summoning the courage to try new things you have never attempted before, or taking chances that set your heart racing. It is important to remain open to new and different ways of doing things—stretching ourselves at times. This is how we grow.

It means making your anger your aid and your ally, instead of an eternal flame that never goes out and eventually consumes you. It means making peace with yourself.

There is nothing to be gained by feeding and nurturing your anger, keeping it alive and well, and allowing it to grow. Doing so only gives it more power. If you are not the master of your anger, you will—sooner or later—become its slave.

By befriending your anger, you set the stage for transformations that may surprise you, and you open a door that can lead you by a more direct route to your goal of healing. It is a challenging thing, but a good thing, well worth trying. May you find this out for yourself and benefit greatly from what you learn.

Things to Think About

1. Typically, when you are angry, what do you do?
2. How angry are you right now about your divorce?
3. If you are angry about it, what is the anger doing to you, and what are you doing with the anger?
4. Can you befriend your anger and channel it into a more positive force in your life? Why or why not?

Forgiving
Your Former Spouse
and Yourself

Loren teaches a class on forgiveness at a local community college, looking mostly at the psychological impact from forgiving or not forgiving someone who has hurt us. The class is always filled to capacity.

"I always start the first class with the story of the wise old woman," he tells his students. "Once upon a time, an old woman lived in the forest. She was known far and wide for her wisdom and kindness to all. One day a stranger came to her home and asked for food. He said he had walked for days without anything to eat, and he was famished. When she opened the cupboard to take out some bread and cheese, he noticed a huge gold nugget next to the food. 'Even more than something to eat,' he said to the old woman, 'I would like to have that gold nugget, for I can sell it and live comfortably for the rest of my life.' She smiled and said, 'You may have both the food and the gold nugget.' The man grabbed them both, then quickly left.

"A few days later he returned. ' Do you need more food?' the old woman asked. 'No,' replied the man. 'I have come for something more important and far more valuable.' 'And what might that be?' the old woman asked. 'I have no more gold.' 'What I seek,' said the man, 'is something I have yearned for all my life. I ask for a portion of that spirit within you that enabled you to freely give me the gold.'

"Within the context of this class," Loren told the students, "we might say that the gold nugget is forgiveness. Lots of people have the capacity for it, but many lack the spirit that enables them to freely give it away. And unless it is given away, it really possesses no value at all."

In recent years, numerous books, journals, and magazines have taken a close look at the power of forgiveness. Once relegated strictly to the domain of religion, it is now viewed as having the ability to positively affect the whole person—physically, psychologically, and spiritually. In fact, we now know that forgiveness heals.

Forgiving someone who has hurt us can heal little hurts as well as big ones. Researchers who have looked at forgiveness scientifically have found that it benefits the heart, the immune system, and the nervous system. Persons suffering from frequent headaches, stomach problems, back pain, and other ailments have found relief through forgiveness. Emotionally, people holding on to grudges that caused them to live in a perpetual state of anger and resentment have gained new freedom through forgiving. That's what happened to Angie.

"When my husband left me for another woman half my age, it's as though my heart turned to ice," she said. "I wished him dead and all kinds of other terrible things. I held on to these feelings for nearly ten years—imagine—an entire decade! I knew it was wrong to hate him, but I savored the hate and didn't want to see it go. It was my constant companion, and it energized me.

At the same time, I developed ulcerative colitis and excruciating headaches. Most of the time I was miserable."

What changed things for her? One Sunday morning, Lauren attended Mass. She remembers that the priest preached about forgiveness. "He talked about the mercy of God who gives us not just a second chance, but a third, fourth, fifth—as many as we want and need." Then, she heard him add: "Whatever we cannot forgive holds us a prisoner and devours us from the inside so that we become the victims of our own unwillingness to forgive." That sermon and the next event changed her life.

When she arrived home after Mass, her three daughters were waiting for her. In Lauren's words, "They did a kind of intervention with me. They told me my lack of forgiveness had poisoned me and the family, and they were sick of it. In my heart, I knew they were right."

What happened next? She smiled as she told me, "I forgave my former husband and his wife. The very next time I saw them, I gave them both a hug. They almost dropped over in the street. I can honestly say that I feel lighter now and more at peace with myself. My ailments are being successfully controlled, and my life is better. I know now that forgiveness really is the right thing to do."

Forgiveness is described in many different ways, but the one I like best says that it is the act of acknowledging—perhaps only to ourselves—that we have been hurt or wronged by someone, yet we consciously and deliberately choose to let go of the desire to get even. It thus becomes a choice, a decision we make.

Many people get confused about forgiveness precisely because they believe it is a feeling. If they don't feel forgiving, then it must not have taken place. But forgiveness is much more than a feeling—feelings after all, can change from minute to minute, hour to hour, day to day. It is really an act of the will we make for ourselves which allows us to decide to forgive.

There is an old saying that feelings are not facts, which is particularly true when it comes to forgiving someone. Feelings of unforgiveness may recur over and over. They do not necessarily mean we haven't forgiven; they do mean that we have to reaffirm our choice once more. Forgiveness can be a process which often goes beyond a one-time decision.

Forgiveness usually happens in several phases. First, we need to be honest with ourselves and acknowledge that we have, indeed, been hurt. This means no more denying that it happened or looking for excuses to explain it away. Someone really did wrong us, maybe even damaged us. Second, it involves a decision to let go of the anger, hatred, and bitterness. This does not mean you excuse the other person's behavior or even that you reconcile with her or him—it takes one person to forgive, it takes two to reconcile. Often, for a variety of reasons, reconciliation is not a possibility. Forgiveness simply means you are ready to let go of the toxic feelings and move on. Third, you actually forgive, even if it is only in your own heart.

Some persons write all their feelings down in a letter that won't ever be sent and forgive the person through the written word. Others begin to pray for the person who hurt them. Do what is best for you and what works for you. Only you need know what has transpired, unless as part of the process, you choose to let the person who wronged you know about what you have done.

What about self-forgiveness? "After I went through my divorce," said Adam, "the person I most detested was me. After all, it was my fault. I had a series of brief flings with other women, and in the process, destroyed my wife's trust and along with her trust, the marriage. I took full blame for the destruction of our marriage, and I was much harder on myself than she was on me. It took a lot of therapy and prayer for me to finally reach the point where I began to forgive myself. I still have to be careful, because when I'm feeling low, I can start reliving the old feelings that nearly destroyed me."

People torture themselves for years because of real or imagined sins, failings, mistakes, or errors in judgment. They may find forgiveness in their hearts for their former spouse yet be unable to forgive themselves.

Refusing to forgive ourselves is a form of self-punishment that deprives us of our own compassion. Without self-forgiveness, we cannot find the inner peace and healing we need after "messing up"—however that is interpreted.

Forgiving ourselves is an important sign of self-love. When we forgive ourselves, we choose to love ourselves just as God has instructed us to do. It is often the only way available to us to purge ourselves of the inner hostility and intense bitterness that can cause so much inner turmoil and take away our sense of peace.

"After my divorce," one man told me, "I used the sacrament of reconciliation over and over again to free me from my feelings of self-hatred and despair that created a kind of inner pain that at times was unbearable. It took awhile, but God's grace began to break through my lack of self-forgiveness, and one day, healing happened. I heard the words deep inside me: 'God loves you and you are forgiven.'"

The feeling of breaking free of the self-loathing awakened him to the self-assurance he needed to love and accept himself again. As he put it, "That was one of the greatest days of my entire life."

What are the benefits of forgiveness, whether it be forgiveness of someone else or yourself? First, forgiving is often the only way to end the inner turmoil which is generated when our emotional and spiritual equilibrium is upset or lost. It is the one way to calm the storms that arise when we cannot let go of rage and resentments. Forgiveness, then, is a way to regain control over our lives.

Second, forgiveness allows us to move on after a failed relationship. It doesn't necessarily solve our relationship problems, but it provides the basis for starting over with trust and hope. It benefits all our relationships, and once experienced, it can be used again and again and become a way of living and relating—an actual lifestyle.

Forgiveness is truly healing. The need for revenge or to get even soaks up a huge amount of emotional and spiritual energy. Forgiveness frees that energy for positive uses. The toxic feelings of anger, guilt, and hurt are drained away by forgiving, and we find ourselves renewed and re-energized. It is liberating.

The Scriptures tell us over and over about God's extravagance when it comes to forgiving us. He asks the same thing of us—that we be generous in forgiving those who have wronged us, as well as in forgiving ourselves.

A divorce can leave many unhealed wounds which continue to hurt. We cannot change the past and what has happened, but we can do something positive about the present and the future. Forgiving can provide a path out of the pain. It is one of the best and most lasting ways to heal a hurting heart.

Things to Think About

1. Is there a need to forgive yourself or some other person associated with your experience of divorce?
2. Do you have a forgiving heart which will allow you to do this?
3. Does it help knowing that forgiveness is more than a feeling?
4. If you cannot forgive right now, can you at least pray for the grace of a forgiving heart?

Letting God Help

As I prepared to write this chapter, I experienced a personal epiphany that I can only describe in this way. In many instances, visiting with persons who had found healing after the experience of divorce became a spiritual experience and source of spiritual enrichment for me. I often felt deeply touched and inspired by their stories of the role faith had played in their lives.

For many, spirituality was clearly a major factor in the healing process following a divorce—perhaps the primary factor. I heard a considerable amount of God-talk and faith sharing in my interviews. In the end, I almost felt like I had made a retreat, with those I interviewed becoming the retreat masters.

For the most part, the persons I talked to were unabashedly spiritual. In this chapter, I will briefly share some of what Rita, Jill, and Mario told me, and you will see what I mean. They spoke freely and openly about the role of their spirituality in the healing process.

Rita had the bluest eyes I had ever seen. She laughed frequently and appeared very much at peace with herself and her post-divorce life. "After six years of marriage," she began, "my husband told me he was gay and was leaving me for another man. I was so shocked that I collapsed right there in our kitchen, and he had to call the paramedics. After the divorce, I was all alone. We had no children, and my parents were deceased, so I said to God: 'It's just you and me. You are the only one I can turn to. Please don't let me down.' He didn't. God had always been a part of my life, but now he became my everything. I have always believed that life is like a classroom that God puts you in to learn certain lessons. Some are easy, some are not. But these experiences are meant to help you grow and grow up, and with the help of God's grace, to become the best person you can be. That is how I eventually came to view my divorce. I said to God, 'Ok, what do you want me to learn from this?' and then I really tried to listen. The lesson he taught me was the most basic one of all. It was all about love. God let me know that just because my ex-husband was gay was not an excuse to stop loving him. Even though I did not like what he had done and was doing, I held fast to the commitment I made to him on our wedding day to love him all the days of my life."

She teared up for a moment, then continued. "Three years after our divorce, he told me he had contracted AIDS. The illness progressed swiftly, and after awhile, I knew he was dying. I invited him to come live with me, and he accepted the invitation. I took care of him until he died. I held his hand while he was dying and was able to tell him I loved him. He told me the same thing. He had a very peaceful death.

"God's ways are not our ways. Letting him into your life means letting in mystery, but always he is the loving mystery who never lets us down. Lives intersect for a reason. I believe that I was meant to take care of my husband, and looking back, I can see that he also took care of me, even when he was dying. It was all about love. It still is."

Jill is an older woman with a gentle smile. She spoke softly and was candid about her experience of divorce. "I was married thirty years before I discovered that my husband had engaged in numerous extramarital affairs almost from the time we were first married. When I learned that he was supporting a mistress, I filed for a divorce. After it was granted, I experienced the worst spiritual crisis of my entire life. I felt unloved by my husband, and I transferred that feeling to God. I began to think that God no longer loved me, because I had divorced my spouse. I saw myself as a great sinner, and I felt condemned in this life and in the next as well. It's true. I despaired of my salvation. It was hell on earth, and, so I believed, hell in the world to come."

What changed things for her? She chuckled as she told me, "Mother Teresa changed things for me. God sent me a saint." Even in the midst of her despair, Jill had remained active in her parish and on a diocesan level. Because of that, she received an invitation to a reception for Mother Teresa, who was visiting her city. Jill emphasized that no one knew what she was thinking or feeling; she hadn't told anyone about her spiritual crisis. "Yet, when I was introduced to Mother Teresa, she looked into my eyes and seemed to see the state of my soul. She hugged me and said, 'My dearest child, God loves you very much. Be at peace.'" Jill was stunned at first. "But then I thought, 'If a saint is telling me God loves me, maybe it is true, and everything I was believing about myself is false.' That was the turning point in my long dark night of the soul. I began to experience some peace, and eventually I healed." Jill now prays an hour each day for those who are divorcing, that they may experience God's love. And she especially asks for Mother Teresa's intercession to pray for them, too. "I believe she is doing just that."

Mario was in his early forties. He had a friendly face and a broad smile. He was wearing a sweatshirt that read: "Stress less, pray more." His story went like this:

"I was married nearly twenty years, and my marriage seemed to be OK. My wife had begun regularly surfing the Internet, meeting different people in chat rooms. She began having regular contact online with a man who lived two thousand miles away—a pretty safe distance, or so I thought. Not so. It happened that she had to get some additional training for her job in a city not far from where he lived. While she was there, they met in person. When she returned home, she informed me that she was leaving. I begged her to stay. I told her I would do anything. I pleaded with her to at least give marriage counseling a chance. She said no to everything, and left. After two years, I filed for a divorce."

He poured us some coffee, as he continued. "I've heard it said that a breakdown can become a breakthrough. That's what happened to me. I reconnected to God. I had been very religious as a young man—even thought of becoming a priest." As Mario grew older, like many young men, he started to drift away from religious practices like going to Mass and praying regularly. He usually only prayed to ask God for help when he needed something.

The divorce, Mario told me, gave him a "real longing for God." That's when he began a daily practice he calls "prayer-walking."

"I would walk for miles, and while I was walking, I would talk to God. Sometimes I would walk and pray the rosary—I didn't care at all if someone saw me. Prayer had become too important to worry about public opinion. Many times I would imagine Jesus walking beside me like he did at Emmaus. I would pour out my heart to him. After awhile, the exercise and the regular prayer started to have a positive effect on both my body and my spirit, and I began to heal."

At the time of our conversation, Mario had begun the process of seeking an annulment, because he hoped to some day remarry in the Church. If he marries again, Mario said, "It's got to be to a woman who loves the Lord and loves to pray. My former wife and I were not all that spiritual together, and I think that had a big influence on our relationship. After all, the greatest intimacy in marriage comes when you and your spouse have a shared faith life and make God a big part of your marriage." Smiling, Mario added, "Now, I know that God is very good for a marriage."

Many of the divorced persons I spoke to were spiritually receptive people. Prayer, for example, had become an important part of their lives. They prayed alone, with others, and for others. Prayer became their lifeline to God.

One woman put it this way: "After my divorce I felt such a need for frequent prayer that I actually took a small room in my home and turned it into a prayer room. I mean a prayer room, and nothing else. It became a sacred space where I would spend time in the morning before going to work and end my day there in the evening. God loves conversation, and so do I. In my prayer room, there is nothing we can't talk about together."

For many divorced persons to whom I spoke, nurturing their faith life and healing from the divorce experience were closely intertwined. Faith was the rudder that steered them unerringly through the worst storms that descended upon them. Their stories deeply affected me, and I still feel that God gently placed his hands upon my life through them.

Based on what I heard in the interviews, I would like to close this chapter with fifteen spiritual principles related to divorce which may be helpful to contemplate, especially when you are spiritually troubled and feel alone in the struggles that have come from your divorce.

- God loves us not just when we are at our best, but even when we are at our worst. Just because you got a divorce does not mean God has stopped loving you.
- Prayer is crucial. Talk to God every day about your life and your situation. Don't hold back. Talk about everything.
- Let go, and let God work in your life in ways he chooses to. Stop telling him what to do and how to do it.
- Forgiving yourself and your former spouse is one of the hardest things you will ever do, but it is one of the most necessary in order to heal.
- Practice the ministry of "holding your tongue." Don't continually badmouth your former spouse or share your dirty laundry with everyone. It makes it harder to heal.
- Nurture your faith life at every opportunity. Go to church, read the Bible and other spiritual material, and find spiritual friends with whom you can grow.
- God is not absent, even if at times he seems to be silent. Trust him.
- An end is also a beginning. Never give up hope that with the help of God's grace, your future can be better than your past.
- Strive for peace, not perfection.
- Do something beautiful for God each day.
- Count your blessings. Don't stop showing your gratitude to God and to others.
- Don't judge.
- Don't let bitterness stop you from loving.

- Remember the healing power of silence. Meditate. Learn to quiet yourself so you can hear God better.
- Your life is a journey toward something greater than this. You have an eternal destiny. Saint Thérèse said: "The world is your ship and not your home." Those words are truer than we may ever imagine.

Things to Think About

1. Spiritually, are you different now than before your divorce? If so, how?
2. Is turning to God a part of your healing process? If not, why not?
3. Is there something you might do to deepen your walk with God? If so, are you willing to do it?

Talking Things Out:
The Benefits of Counseling

—

Father Dennis is the spiritual advisor to a divorce support group that meets regularly at his parish. He often stresses to them the importance of talking things out. The night I attended, among other things, he told them this:

"When a marriage ends, for most people it is a significant loss, and that means there will be grieving. When we begin the journey of grief, we need a buddy to walk with us—someone we trust completely and can unburden ourselves to. We need to be able to put our strongest and rawest feelings into words and know those words have been heard by her or him and that we will not be judged or criticized for saying them. This person can't fix us or make us okay, but he or she can be with us in our pain. "

He continued. "The Bible tells us that it is not good to be alone. God has made us social creatures who do better when we have someone to talk to and listen to us. Talking about our problems makes us stronger, not weaker. It helps us find the insights we need to go on and create a new life for ourselves. It is a way to open the windows of our soul to healing."

For many persons, life after divorce is turbulent. A host of feelings besiege us, all demanding expression. New goals may present themselves which need to be prioritized. Decisions have to be made about the present and the future. It is usually a time when one's plate is plenty full.

We live in a society that extols the virtues of rugged individualism and fosters a can-do sort of attitude. This attitude urges us to take charge of our own lives and solve our problems by ourselves through sheer determination and disciplined will-power.

The problem is that sooner or later many people recognize that they need help. They become tired of battling a host of problems all by themselves.

Talking things out with another person can be of great help, especially during times of transition when major life changes are occurring. Who should you talk to? It's really up to you. That person may be a close friend, a pastor, or a colleague. However, many people benefit from talking to a professional counselor.

Surveys done by the American Psychological Association have found that at least one person in nearly half of all the households in the United States has seen a mental health professional, and nine out of ten of those surveyed indicated the counseling helped them. Even those who went for only a few sessions said they were better off than if they had received no counseling at all.

If you had told Glen that one day he would be in counseling, he would have laughed. "I'm not crazy, and I don't need a shrink," would have been his response. But after his divorce he began to experience considerable anxiety along with flashbacks of the fifteen months he spent in Iraq.

"After awhile," he said, "I knew I needed help. One day I called the local VA hospital and set up an appointment with a counselor. He told me during the very first session that I had post-traumatic stress disorder made worse by all the stress from my divorce. He helped me a lot. I started out seeing him every week, but now, it's only once a month or so. I still look forward to those sessions, though. It allows me to get things off my chest."

Counseling—also called therapy—is a very broad term used to describe a variety of disciplines and approaches that address psychological, social, and behavioral issues. A counselor or therapist is a trained expert who helps others take an honest look at their lives. Areas of concern may include, for example, depression or other emotional disorders, personal relationships, goals, and career development. Anything the person seeking counseling wants to talk about is fair game.

Alex, a licensed professional counselor (LPC), had this to say about his profession. "People who have counseled with me commonly say things like, 'You helped me get my act together,' or 'I'm functioning better now at work and at home,' or 'I'm handling stress better now.' I see myself empowering them to discover the insights and develop the skills that will make their life's journey happier and more fulfilling. Counseling is not magic. It does not provide a quick fix, nor does it make our lives perfect. But it can make them better by improving our emotional health."

Simply put, counseling is talk therapy done in a safe, secure, and confidential environment. The counselor or therapist listens and then uses his or her professional expertise to explore root causes of psychological, social, or behavioral problems. Talk therapy generally helps persons better understand their problems and look for positive ways to address them.

Many different kinds of mental-health professionals are skilled in counseling. For example, a psychiatrist is a physician trained to treat mental disorders. Psychiatrists utilize talk therapy and may also prescribe medications for psychiatric illnesses such as depression or anxiety. Seeing a psychiatrist is a good idea when it is clear the patient has a mental disorder that will require medication to successfully treat it.

Psychologists typically have a doctorate or a master's degree. They are skilled in applying psychological principles to emotional and behavioral disorders.

Clinical social workers also have a doctorate or master's degree and are trained to provide counseling. They often emphasize how interpersonal relationships and community factors impact the individual's ability to function in a healthy way.

Licensed professional counselors have a minimum of a master's degree and are licensed by the state in which they practice. Their training is similar to that of a psychologist and clinical social worker.

Marriage and family therapists focus on helping couples and families develop stronger communication skills and healthier ways of interacting that strengthen relationships.

What kind of counselor or therapist should you select? The training received by those described above is basically quite similar. No evidence shows one kind of counselor is superior to another. Choosing one will likely depend on where you live, recommendations you receive from others who have been in therapy, and your own unique needs.

Sometimes two different branches of the psychotherapeutic field feel the need to collaborate to help a person struggling with mental health issues. So, for example, a psychiatrist may treat a patient with serious depression with medication but may also recommend that the patient see a psychologist or clinical social worker for talk therapy. In this way the two work together for the person's well-being.

Although most counselors utilize similar techniques, mental-health practitioners are often trained in a particular school of thought which influences the way they approach therapy.

Cognitive therapists, for example, look at the patient's patterns of thinking. They challenge erroneous or impaired patterns and help the patient develop healthier, more positive ones. Behavioral therapists deal directly with symptoms such as stress and use mental techniques and exercises to help the person manage them better. Substance-abuse counselors confront the misuse of drugs and alcohol and may even recommend hospitalization as part of the rehabilitation process.

A counselor or therapist is a mental-health professional, yet it is important to note that most who seek counseling are not mentally ill. Sickness is not an issue for them. They come to counseling seeking help for excessive stress, loneliness, new life situations, traumatic experiences, or grief issues—all of which can be as incapacitating as a mental illness.

"A week after my divorce was final," said Leo, "My father and my brother were killed together in a car accident. My pastor told me I needed to see a professional counselor to help get me through what became the worst period of my entire life. The first thing the counselor did was help me realize that I wasn't going crazy. I was having a grief reaction, and the bizarre feelings I was experiencing were normal. She provided me with a new way of looking at my grief which helped me a great deal. I knew that I could tell her anything and everything about what I was going through, and believe me, I did."

Is there still a stigma attached to seeing a counselor? Things have gotten better, but sometimes because of their own lack of knowledge or misinformation, some are quick to judge those who seek counseling. Sadly, there are also those who believe that counseling is for "crazy" people or for "weak" people who can't get their act together and can't handle their own problems. Others may dismiss counseling as a crutch or a waste of time and money.

Don't listen to them.

Your life, your well-being, and your opinion matter most, so do what you believe is best for you. Remember that counseling does not have to be a long-term commitment. Sometimes, even a few sessions can make a big difference.

In conclusion, we all experience times in our lives when we long to be listened to and be given honest, truthful, and helpful feedback on what we say. That is what counseling is all about. You enter a relationship with a trained professional in which you can express your deepest thoughts and feelings in a safe setting and work on issues together.

Counseling can be especially beneficial before, during, and after the turbulence of divorce. Benefits can include improved relationships, personal growth, and maturation—and a happier, healthier, more satisfying life. Counseling is not a quick fix for problems and can actually be hard, painful work at times, but the benefits generally far outweigh the demands involved.

Many people who have experienced a divorce have found solace and peace through talking things out. Whether it be with a professional counselor or someone else, may your communication experience be positive and good and lead you closer to the goal of healing.

Things to Think About

1. Do you talk regularly to someone you trust about your experience of divorce?
2. If you do, is it helpful? If you don't, why not?
3. Have you considered professional counseling? If not, would this be a good time to start?

Healing Through
Service to Others

—————

I sat down with Lucy one Saturday morning to listen to her experience of divorce. I was aware of some of her story, because she had been married to a man I once worked with. I knew that he had a serious drinking problem, but as we talked, she revealed to me that he had been abusive as well.

These factors and others had made their twelve-year marriage extremely troubled and unhappy for her. But now, two years after her divorce, she looked happy and serene. When I asked her what had helped her heal, she smiled and said: "Let me tell you a story.

"It seems that a holy man was at prayer one day when he asked God to show him what heaven and hell were like. Immediately, he found himself standing in front of two closed doors. He opened the first one and saw people sitting around a large round table. In the middle of the table was a big pot of the most delicious-smelling stew imaginable, yet every person at the table looked emaciated and unhappy. In each of their hands was a pair of chopsticks, at least five feet long. They could reach into the pot of stew and get some food, but because of the length of the chopsticks, they could not get the food back into their mouths. Their frustration and hunger clearly made them unbearably miserable.

"The holy man knew immediately that he had just seen a vision of hell. He opened the next door and looked inside. The room was exactly like the first one with the same large round table and the stew pot in the middle. The people around this table also had pairs of long-handled chopsticks, but they looked well-nourished and happy. The holy man knew he was seeing heaven, yet he wondered what it was that made the all-important difference between the two places. Then, as he watched, in an instant he understood. In heaven, he saw the people using their chopsticks to feed each other across the table."

Lucy sipped her coffee; then she said to me: "I have learned the joy of feeding others. In my case, *literally* feeding others. After my divorce, I joined the staff of our local soup kitchen, and I was put in charge of the children's after-school program. I make sure that nearly five hundred hungry kids get a sandwich, a cookie, and some milk after their school day is over. And in the giving comes the receiving. They give back to me far more than I could ever give them, but by helping others, I have also helped myself. That is one of the big reasons for my personal healing."

Others I spoke to echoed what Lucy told me, namely, that serving love had played a big part in helping them recover from their divorces. By helping others, they also helped themselves.

One woman who decided to become a nurse after her divorce quoted Mother Teresa to me: "'It's not how much we give, but how much love we put into giving,'" she said. Then she added this: "I became a nurse for two reasons. First, I received no alimony and very little child support. I needed a job I could count on to support me and my children. But equally important, I wanted a job that was also a ministry. With nursing, I can earn enough money to take care of myself and my family, and I can also be a vessel of God's love to the sick. It's a win-win situation."

When people talked to me about the positive effects of serving others after their divorce, they often brought up another aspect of how they were affected. Serving love appeared to play an instrumental role in changing the kinds of dark, negative attitudes that were blocking their healing. When they reached out to others and gave of themselves, things began to change for the better. Here is what Leon had to say:

"Yes, I can honestly say that helping others brought about an attitude adjustment in me. My former wife used to call me a 'negaholic.' She would say that I always saw the glass as half empty, not half full. I would focus on what was wrong with her and wrong with our marriage and not stop criticizing. I'm ashamed to say now that my attitudes very much affected our marriage and were a big reason why she finally left me.

"After our divorce, I had enough sense to get some therapy. The therapist helped me see how I looked at the world through dark-colored glasses. She suggested that I find some way to help others in need. It just so happened that in my parish bulletin I saw a note saying that eucharistic ministers were needed to take Communion to the local hospital. At first, I didn't want to do it, but a little nagging voice in my head would not let up. I think that might have been God."

He continued. "I've been a hospital eucharistic minister now for the past four years, and it really has changed me for the better. Ministering to the sick, especially the dying, made me realize pretty quickly how blessed I am and how small my problems are. More than that, I started meeting seriously ill patients who ministered to me, who were kind and caring and wanted to know how I was, and who promised to pray for me. Their love for me began to change me, and I consciously made an effort to be more loving and less negative myself."

Leon chuckled. "It must have been a change for the better, because my former wife and I are now dating again, and there's a good possibility we may remarry each other. She tells me that I'm different, and I guess I am. I don't want to go back to the way I was. I didn't like myself very much back then, but I do now, and it shows."

There is something healing and restorative about actively promoting the well-being and happiness of others. It makes us feel good about ourselves, perhaps in part because we become less preoccupied with our own problems and concerns. Rosemarie put it this way:

"The most significant person in my life was a nun named Sister Barbara. She taught high school religion, and more than just teaching religion, she lived out her beliefs in the ways she treated people. She was fond of saying, 'Remember, love isn't love until you give it away.' Sister Barbara was probably the most loving person I have ever known. When I married, I tried to bring as much love as I could to the relationship I had with my husband, but he couldn't accept it. After trying for ten years to bond with him, I realized it would never happen, because he was mentally ill; I would be mentally ill myself if I stayed with him any longer. Reluctantly, I sought a divorce.

"But Sister Barbara was always there in the back of my mind, reminding me to give my love away. One day while I was praying, I asked God how I could best do this, and the answer came immediately from the very depths of my soul—do it the way she did. Become a nun, too."

She smiled broadly. "So now I'm Sister Rosemarie, and let me tell you, God has a sense of humor. I am teaching high school religion in the same school I attended and where Sister Barbara also once taught. The school is now in the inner city, and most of my students are poor, but they have great potential and a willingness to learn. Every day, before I enter the classroom, I quietly say to the children inside waiting, 'I love you, I love you, I love you,' then I go in, and love them into learning. Only God could turn something like a divorce into a wonderful new life, where the more you give, the more you *have* to give. I am blessed beyond measure."

A point I need to emphasize before we continue is that finding healing through service does not mean we completely ignore our own needs in order to meet the needs of others. To do so leads to codependency, which only makes our situation more dysfunctional. Nor should our goal be to make others indebted to us so that we expect something back in return.

The people I spoke to who were doing well had achieved some level of emotional and spiritual equilibrium. Meeting their own needs *and* the needs of others were pretty much in balance, and they were learning to give without counting the cost or keeping a record for future repayment.

We all have needs that will not go away, nor should they. What service does is not teach us to ignore our needs, but to become less preoccupied with them. Serving others can shift our focus from ourselves and reduce our tendency to become self-centered. It allows us to look at life from a different perspective.

Practicing serving love can make us aware that there are other people in need, not just us, and that Christ who came to serve and not be served expects some kind of outreach to them. How we do this depends on our own unique gifts and resources. The opportunities to help are legion; the response is always up to us based on our discernment.

Are you looking for ways to be of service following your divorce? Many organizations are looking for volunteers to do a multitude of things that will benefit other people. You can start with your church. Most churches are grateful for new help, which is often much-needed and much-appreciated. Schools use volunteers to tutor their students, and hospitals use volunteers in myriad ways—everything from passing out mail to distributing Communion, like Leon does. Soup kitchens are always in need of more help. Find a place that can put your gifts to good use, then get started.

An important way to serve is through the language we use. Words have power to hurt or heal. Saying the right things at the right time can be enormously healing. For example, practice the ministry of encouragement. There are people all around us who feel discouraged and defeated by life. Bolster their spirits at every opportunity. Say or do something that brings them encouragement and hope. Anything that you can do to lessen their burdens is a valuable form of service that can have far-reaching consequences. Praise is another verbal way to practice serving love. People all around us have been damaged by too much criticism and not enough affirmation—a word which comes from the Latin meaning "to make strong." We can make others stronger by our words of praise and affirmation. Even a simple sincere compliment can boost another person's spirit.

Small deeds are important forms of service. The fact is that in life there are few opportunities to render service in a big way. Great opportunities seldom come along, but each day brings ample opportunities for small acts of love. Little acts of service can take such forms as providing snow removal for an elderly person, giving someone a ride to church, inviting a family struggling financially to dinner, listening with understanding and compassion to another unburden himself or herself , or gifting someone with a warm smile. The Scriptures tell us clearly that God takes small acts of kindness and multiplies them into something significant. We can all serve others in little ways. Little things we do can lead to big results.

Happiness is seldom found by pursuing it directly. It usually comes to us as a byproduct of loving and serving others. In helping others, we also help ourselves, and the first step toward healing following a great loss such as the end of your marriage is to reach out to another with serving love. Try it, and see for yourself.

Things to Think About

1. Is service of others important to you? Why or why not?
2. When was the last time you tried to help someone in need? What happened?
3. Today, could you do three small acts of service for others?

Laughter Is Good Medicine

Stan and Eileen ended their marriage in a positive way—with laughter. Plenty of laughter. Stan described what happened: "We had a very amicable divorce, and I wanted to keep things positive between us. So, a few weeks after everything was finalized, I invited Eileen to dinner just to reminisce. And over a bottle of wine—maybe two—that's what we did. We took turns telling funny, happy stories about our marriage, and we laughed and laughed. It was so good an experience that we repeated it several times. I wanted to remain on friendly terms with Eileen, and laughing together helped achieve that."

Eileen spoke in a similar way. "It's hard to stay mad at one another when you both laugh together. Laughter makes everything seem better, more manageable, less serious. Many couples who are divorcing can't stop focusing on all the pain and hurt they've inflicted on each other—all the hard times. Stan and I had plenty of those, too, but when we look back on our sixteen years of marriage, we choose to emphasize the positive. And there are plenty of funny stories to keep us in stitches for a long time to come. Recently, at our daughter's wedding, we both told hilarious stories about raising her that had the guests rolling on the floor. Laughter made that wedding extra special, and it has made our divorce better than I ever thought it would be."

"When it comes to dealing with a divorce," one man told me, "life doesn't provide you with an instruction manual. You learn as you go along." Many of the persons I interviewed alluded to learning about the power of laughter, of loosening up, of not taking things quite so seriously. Said one woman, divorced four years, "If I didn't laugh, I would cry. Actually, many times I did both, but I certainly prefer the laughter." Added a man, newly divorced, "If I can laugh at it, I can live with it."

There is an old Russian saying that to really understand God, we must learn to love change...and a joke. The Book of Proverbs is also right on target when it says that "a lighthearted person has a continual feast" (Proverbs 15:15). Laughter, good humor, fun, joy—all of these are fundamentally spiritual qualities that possess the ability to harness soul power and put it to work. They don't necessarily solve our problems, but they can help us rise above our circumstances and view things in a different way, a lighter way.

It became clear to me that when persons going through the experience of divorce were able to laugh, in that brief moment, they found hope, wholeness, and temporarily some release from the tumult divorce can bring.

Above all, humor was a sign that they had not given up—even when times became painful. For such persons, laughter became a rallying cry that they would not only survive their divorce, they would thrive. They would rebuild and have a life again.

Being able to laugh emphasized their strengths, not their weaknesses. It underscored what was productive in their lives instead of the unproductive. For Ed and Bonnie, that meant drawing on the joy of being parents and having three wonderful children. "We decided early on in our divorce," said Bonnie, "that we were going to remain friendly for their sake. Laughter had always been a big part of our home life for a long time. We wanted to continue that, and we have."

"When we get together with the kids," Ed added, "there are plenty of funny stories, joking, and good-natured teasing. All in all, it's a great deal of fun. It's good for the kids and good for us. It has helped ease some of the stress from the divorce and made the transition to a new way of relating as a family much easier."

Trying to see the humor even in something as serious as a divorce and laughing even in the midst of problems have been shown repeatedly in scientific research to benefit the whole person, body, mind, and spirit. Here are a few ways that happens.

A good laugh not only provides a physical and emotional release, it increases hormones that strengthen the body's immune system, thereby providing some protection from some of the stress a divorce can bring.

Laughing has been described as "internal jogging." It actually is very much like getting some of the benefits that exercise brings, including the release of those special chemicals in the brain called endorphins, which make us feel good after a workout and contribute to a feeling of well-being.

Laughter has even been found to be good for the heart. It enhances the way blood vessels expand and improves blood flow, thereby lowering the chance of a heart attack or stroke. In other words, a happy heart is a healthier heart.

Laughter can alter our perspective on events taking place in our lives, helping us to view them in a more positive light. If we see certain events as threats, we are more likely to activate what is often called the "fight or flight response," which puts our body on red alert and readies us to respond to some impending danger before us.

On the other hand, if we can laugh at what is looming before us and reduce its emotional impact, in effect, we defuse a potential crisis, making it less menacing and more manageable. Our body is thus spared the expenditure of great emotional and physical energy it normally would use to protect us.

Finally, laughter has important social dynamics. Have you ever been in a theater where the entire audience is howling at the show? Everyone feels bonded. There is a connection taking place that only laughter can bring about, and the more laughing, the better everyone feels.

Therefore, when you make other people laugh, they benefit from the same effects discussed earlier, and you benefit, too. It's a win-win situation. Simply put, laughter improves the quality of social interactions and helps people relate to one another in more positive ways.

So, laughter does good things to us and for us. It is beneficial for the whole human race.

Charles had this to say about the subject of laughter and divorce. "I remember the day my lawyer and I were meeting with my soon-to-be ex-wife and her attorney. I had fallen earlier in the week and had injured my leg. I felt crummy and just wanted everything to be over, but we had hit an impasse, and nothing was happening."

He continued. "I popped a couple of aspirin, and as I did so, I recalled something my father used to say: 'I have learned that just because I have pain, I don't have to be one.' I shared his saying with the other three, everyone laughed, and what do you know—that broke up the logjam. We were out of the room in ten minutes. I learned that day that even a small amount of humor can go a very long way when it comes to the divorce process.

"In fact, he added, "if I ruled the world, I would mandate that every divorcing couple and their lawyers would be required to sit down together and watch three Marx Brothers movies, complete with popcorn and soda, before proceeding with the heavy-duty stuff of a divorce. I call it my 'belly-laugh' approach to a divorce settlement, and I'm willing to bet that it would do a lot more good and be more effective than the system we currently have."

Angie, a former divorce attorney, knows the value of a healthy ability to laugh. "I worked with many clients over the years, and I can honestly say that the couples that laughed together seemed to do better and resolved their issues more quickly. Laughter wasn't necessarily a panacea that solved all their problems, but it did have a way of evaporating a lot of hostility and anger so that they could address the real issues without the negative emotions getting in the way. When God put the capacity for laughter into each of us, he knew what he was doing. In fact, he was probably laughing himself as he did it."

One important caveat, when it comes to laughter and humor: keep it all appropriate. What I mean by that is that making your former spouse an object of ridicule or the butt of your jokes is inappropriate and wrong. Ridiculing her or him is really a form of getting even and getting back for real or imaginary wrongs. When we laugh at the expense of somebody else's feelings, we are being spiteful and mean. This is the very antithesis of the healing process, and it actually impedes it for you and for your former spouse.

Sarcasm as an attempt at being funny is even worse. Sarcasm comes from two Greek words which mean "to cut the flesh." When we are pretending to be humorous but are really being sarcastic, our intent is basically hostile, namely, to use words as knives to cut her or him to pieces. Nothing good can come of that.

"I always prided myself on being a funny man," Derrick confided to me. "I could keep a room full of people in stitches with my jokes and routines, especially my impersonations. My divorce left me extremely bitter, and looking back now, I can see how I used humor to hurt my former wife. I would tell really mean jokes about her and do impersonations of her in embarrassing situations. I depicted her as fat and ugly, and I proclaimed to anyone who would listen that she would never remarry, because no one would ever want someone who looked the way she did."

What changed things for Derrick? "Our diocese sponsored a retreat for divorced persons, and I went. The speaker was powerful. It was as though he knew me through and through, although we had never met before. When he spoke about the need to continue loving our former spouses, even though we may not like them, I really listened. He said that one way we can express our love is by being careful with our gift of speech and not using it to keep a heated guerrilla war alive and well with them."

He continued. "I knew that is exactly what I had been doing—using humor to bait her and then hurt her. That weekend, I made a decision to stop it, and I pretty well have. On occasion, I slip and say something sarcastic about her, but for the most part, my attempts at humor reflect the attitude adjustment I experienced on that retreat."

Laughter can be good medicine when it is used as part of the healing process following a divorce. People heal more quickly when they find things they can laugh about. It is a path well-worth taking and trying. If you do, may it bring you closer to your goal of peace of heart and new wholeness.

Things to Think About

1. Do you have a sense of humor, and if so, how would you describe it?
2. Can you find anything humorous in your experience of divorce?
3. Is it possible for you to draw upon your sense of humor to cope better with your divorce? Why or why not?
4. Can you enjoy a hearty laugh today?

Self Care and Self Healing

———

I f there was one theme I heard over and over again in my interviews related to healing after a divorce, it was that of self-care.
Virtually everyone I talked to in one way or another spoke of
the need to take care of yourself or healing might not happen.

"A divorce tears you up inside," Warren, a forty-two-year-old
man, divorced for three years, told me. "It clobbers you good.
You don't need to add to the damage by burning the candle at
both ends and exhausting yourself in the process. Listen to me,
I know all about it. I started working seven days a week after my
divorce was over. I lost myself in my work, so I wouldn't have to
deal with all the inner pain. What I discovered was that the pain
was patiently waiting for me, biding its time. So, when I got laid
off from my job, it pounced on me, and after awhile, I hurt so
bad I felt I had nothing to live for. I was actually thinking more
and more about ending it all, when my union began a series of
stress management classes related to job loss. I felt I had nothing
more to lose, so I went."

What did Warren learn? " I learned a lot from the classes. I
especially learned that you have to take care of yourself. That's
the bottom line. You've got to commit yourself to it. If you don't,
no one is going to do it for you. Self-care is self-preservation."

Burnout was a topic which came up often in our conversations. A number of persons talked about crashing and burning—getting so depleted that they were unable to function in a normal, healthy way.

The danger signs that point to burnout include: deep exhaustion and fatigue that refuses to go away, depression, episodes of anger and irritability, physical complaints, a change in sleeping and eating habits, loss of a sense of pleasure, diminished contact with family and friends, forgetfulness, and loss of a sense of humor.

Marcie put it this way. "Following my divorce, I started to get more and more cynical and less fun to be with. People would say to me, 'Hey, you've changed. You're not the same person you once were.' It was true. The joy had evaporated from my life. I knew I needed help, but until I asked for it, not much happened to change things."

The advice I heard was to learn how to hit the brakes before reaching the kind of burnout Marcie and others experienced. What that means is regular, ongoing self care, not just an occasional reward every now and then.

Based on what I heard, I offer these observations and suggestions related to self care following the experience of divorce.

First, you must make self care a priority. The decision to take care of yourself and your needs is seldom made once-and-for-all. It usually needs to be made over and over again. With all the turbulence and turmoil associated with a divorce, it is easy to leave self care behind in the dust and turn your attention to other concerns.

But self care is a big deal. It is important, necessary, and it is worth all the effort to make it happen. Don't let it become another casualty of your divorce.

Taking care of yourself comes about through making choices. We change by choosing. The persons I spoke to told me that they sometimes had to make hard choices in order for self care to happen, but they felt those choices were justified and worth it. Self care is a recognition and affirmation of the fact that you have needs, too, and that you deserve to have at least some of those needs met.

Creating ways for you to refill your cup is not wrong; it is a necessity. You need not feel guilty about taking care of yourself. It is really a manifestation of self love. When Jesus talked about loving our neighbor as we love ourselves, he meant it, or he would not have said it. If God wants us to love ourselves, then clearly that must make it something good.

Learning how to take care of ourselves and our needs is really the work of a lifetime, but it takes on special meaning following a divorce. Then, we especially need to identify and utilize those resources available to us that renew and refresh us emotionally, spiritually, and physically.

For example, a significant number of the people I interviewed stressed the importance of exercise. Regular exercise has a way of burning off stress, relieving frustrations and tensions, and dispelling some of the more negative emotions that can assault our minds. Even if we feel good, exercise makes us feel better.

Ray had this to say about exercise following his divorce. "I didn't have a lot of money after I divorced, but I knew that sitting around in my apartment watching television night after night or making the rounds of the bars was suffocating me. I needed to get my blood flowing in order to feel alive again. So, I cut back on some of my expenses like eating out, and I joined a gym. The change was almost immediate. I started feeling better about myself, looking better, and thinking more positively. I would come home rejuvenated, whereas when I was hitting the bars, I came home depressed. My advice to someone going through a divorce or already divorced: Get plenty of exercise. Don't miss a day. It's a medicine that works and works very well."

What constitutes self care besides exercise? Practically anything and everything. In my interviews, I heard a wide variety of descriptions of self care. Many persons, for example, stressed the ordinary things like getting enough rest along with proper nutrition. Some, however, had fashioned more creative approaches to self care.

"The nights being all alone were the hardest things for me to deal with after my divorce," said Jason. "The loneliness made me agitated, and I kept looking for ways to calm my restless spirit. Then, one day, I remembered an old childhood dream I had never fulfilled. As a kid I had always wanted to study the stars but never had enough money to buy a good telescope."

He laughed and said, "Now, look at me. I'm a stargazer." He pointed to the large telescope in his living room. "Almost every night I spend time studying the heavens. I even discovered a comet, which has been named after me. When you spend a lot of time looking into the face of the universe, it changes your perspective on life. My spirit is more serene now than it has ever been."

Jessica said: "For me self care took the form of going back to school. From the time I was five years old, I knew I wanted to teach kindergarten, but I never got the chance to finish college. After my divorce, I decided it's now or never, so I resumed my education. I've been teaching kindergarten for the past ten years, and I can't tell you how much joy and fulfillment it has brought to me."

Sally told me: "I have a bipolar disorder—some people still call it manic depressive illness. I also have a doctorate in psychology. For me, self-care has meant going around to various organizations like the PTA, service clubs like Rotary, and church groups, and sharing my experience with this illness. Most people don't have the foggiest idea what bipolar disorder is really like, and my goal is to educate and inform them. I also run a support group made up of other adults who are bipolar like me. It's a safe haven where everyone can share without being judged. Since my divorce, this group has become a healing place in a hurting world for me."

Donna had another story: "At the time of my divorce, I was a very successful attorney. I still liked my work, but I also had a nagging feeling that something was missing, and I knew what it was. At age fifty, I started medical school. At age fifty-six, as a brand-new doctor, I opened a clinic in one of the poorest counties in America. Now I work much longer hours than when I was practicing law, but it seems I am never really tired. I love what I am doing so much that it keeps me energized and joyous."

There is no one-size-fits-all kind of self care program. What works for one person may not work for another. If we tailor self-care to our unique needs, our temperament, and the resources available to us, we are more likely to stick to it and reap the kinds of benefits from it that are truly restorative.

The stress associated with a divorce tends to be formidable. Self care becomes an important part of self protection that can prevent burnout from occurring.

The challenge, then, is to do whatever we can to take care of ourselves, no matter how small it may be. Remember that even little successes count. They can make us feel less helpless and hopeless and help us realize we are still in charge of our own lives.

"When I feel overwhelmed, I just lie on the couch and listen to my favorite music," one man told me. "After awhile, I calm down, and life looks better again. I heal one song at a time."

Take good care of yourself. Healing is something you deserve.

Things to Think About

1. When it comes to self care, are you doing enough for yourself? If not, why not?
2. If you were to try some different forms of self care, what would they be?
3. What is the single best way you have of refilling your cup? When was the last time you did it?
4. Do you view self care as a form of self love? Why or why not?

Closing Thoughts

———

I am ending this book with a presumption. I presume that you have read this book because you have been hurt and wounded by your experience of divorce, and now you are in need of healing.

The message of this book is that healing can and does happen. It has happened to many others—some of whose stories I have told here—and it can happen to you.

Whether you take any one of the eight paths I have described, all of them, or some other path, the important thing is that you keep working on your recovery. In fact, it is possible that you are already closer to that goal than you may realize, so do not lose heart.

You start the healing process by first choosing to heal. Healing is always the first choice we need to make. It then becomes the starting point for everything else. It is courage that gives us the strength to choose.

Your life has been changed by the divorce—perhaps radically changed—but you can choose to do more than survive. You can actually thrive. Your spirit wants to thrive and to be whole again. Listen carefully to what it is telling you.

Strange as it may seem, there may actually be something valuable in the pain you have experienced. There may be a gift in it not only for you, but also for others. With the help of God's grace, we can become empowered to transform even our deepest pain into something good—even beautiful—something loving and lasting.

You have an appointment with life—*your* life. Don't miss it. May you embrace your journey and go forward in peace to fulfill your destiny and celebrate the joy of you.

I wish you the best of blessings.

Other Titles on Divorce and Recovery

Prayers for Catholics Experiencing Divorce
Revised Edition

In this updated and revised edition of *Prayers for Catholics Experiencing Divorce* are forty-four prayers to help Catholics experiencing divorce heal the hurt as they rediscover themselves and their self-worth.

96-page paperback • ISBN 978-0-7648-1156-2

Making Your Way After Your Parents' Divorce
A Supportive Guide for Personal Growth

Written by a "child of divorce" for "children of divorce," *Making Your Way After Your Parents' Divorce* takes an honest look at the effects that divorce can have in the life of a teenager or young adult, and the ways that they can move toward healing and forgiveness after their parents' divorce. Although aimed at teenagers and young adults, this book is a valuable resource for counselors, ministers, religious educators, social workers, and divorced parents themselves. Ideal for both individual and group use.

128-page paperback • ISBN 978-0-7648-0872-2

Regaining Joy
A Guide to Overcoming Stress and Sadness

Millions of people suffer from depression that requires clinical treatment. But many others live with a subtle, yet pervasive sense of sadness and joylessness in their lives. This little book helps transform those feelings through understanding what is going on, honest prayer, and resolutions to live more joyfully and hopefully. There are many self-help types of books on depression, but few are set in the form of short, prayerful reflections. *Regaining Joy* is for those who fear they may be on the edge of falling into depression or experience a chronic state of sadness and joylessness.

80-page paperback • ISBN 978-0-7648-1580-5

For prices and ordering information, call us toll free at 800-325-9521 or visit our Web site, www.liguori.org.